Sci√m

THE SCIENCE MUSEUM BOOK OF AMAZING FACTS

SPACE

Dr Anthony Wilson is a writer and teacher who has followed developments in astronomy and space exploration for many years. He can even remember when the first satellite, Sputnik 1, was launched - and that was in 1957! For many years he was Head of Education at the Science Museum in London, where he set up the popular hands-on gallery Launch Pad. He is now helping start a new Hands-on Science Centre in a one-time astronomical observatory at Herstmonceux in Sussex.

The amazing facts in this book were inspired by exhibits in the SCIENCE MUSEUM in London. It is home to many of the greatest treasures in the history of science, invention and discovery, and there are also hands-on galleries where you can try things out for yourself. If you live in the North of England visit the Science Museum's outposts, the National Railway Museum in York and the National Museum of Photography, Film & Television in Bradford.

Published by Hodder Children's Books 1996
The right of Anthony Wilson to be identified as the Author and
the right of Jane Cope to be identified as the Illustrator of the Work
has been asserted by them in accordance with the
Copyright, Designs and Patents Act 1988

10 9 8 7 6 5 4 3 2

A Catalogue record for this book is available
from the British Library

ISBN 0-340-65696 4

Designed by Fiona Webb
Cover illustration by Ainslie MacLeod

Hodder Children's Books
A division of Hodder Headline plc
338 Euston Road
London NW1 3BH

Printed and bound in Great Britain by
Cox & Wyman, Reading, Berks.

THE SCIENCE MUSEUM
BOOK OF AMAZING FACTS

SPACE

ANTHONY WILSON
ILLUSTRATED BY JANE COPE

*Hodder
Children's
Books*

a division of Hodder Headline plc

Contents

A MATTER OF SOME GRAVITY

Everyone has felt the force of gravity – even though a famous scientist said that it doesn't exist. You'll meet gravity many times in this book. It is the force that pulls things to the ground when you drop them. The Earth's gravity stops us falling off the planet, keeps spacecraft in orbit, and stops the Moon flying away into space. The Sun's gravity holds the Earth and other planets on course and keeps comets in their long, thin orbits. Every single thing that exists exerts a pull of gravity on everything else, but the pull is usually too small to notice except when we're close to a massive object like the Earth. But according to one of the greatest scientists who has ever lived, Albert Einstein, gravity isn't a real force at all. It is just the result of space being curved!

A BILLION - BIG OR SMALL?

A billion is a big number in everyday life, but a small number for astronomers. If 10,000 people go to a football match, the number of hairs on all their heads adds up to about a billion. And a billion is about the number of times your heart will beat in the next 25 years. But in talking about planets, stars and the universe, a billion doesn't stretch very far. A billion kilometres from Earth doesn't even get you out of the Solar System, and a billion years isn't even a quarter of the age of the Earth. You will meet a lot of billions in this book.

CHAPTER 1
Going into Space

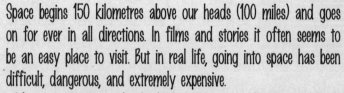

Space begins 150 kilometres above our heads (100 miles) and goes on for ever in all directions. In films and stories it often seems to be an easy place to visit. But in real life, going into space has been difficult, dangerous, and extremely expensive.

Like a giant magnet, the Earth clings onto everything around it. To overcome the planet's strong gravity, huge rockets are needed to lift things off the ground and boost them into orbit. The first satellite – a tiny man-made moon in orbit round the Earth – was launched in 1957. Since then thousands of larger satellites have followed it into orbit, and many of them are still there.

Sending humans into space is even harder than sending satellites, because humans need so many aids to keep them alive there. They must be given food and drink, and air to breathe. Their spacecraft must protect them from dangerous radiation and from scorching sunlight and bitter cold.

Today the Space Shuttle, part rocket and part aeroplane, makes regular trips into orbit. If you ever go into space yourself, you will probably travel by Shuttle, or on some future rocket-plane that takes off and lands at an airport.

UTTER BILGE

'Space travel is utter bilge.' The most important astronomer in England - the 'Astronomer Royal' - said these words in 1956. One year later the first artificial satellite, Sputnik 1, went up. Thirteen years later, humans walked on the Moon. The astronomer, Richard van der Riet Woolley, wasn't the first person to be caught out by saying something would never happen. A very famous physicist, Ernest Rutherford, once said that anyone who thought nuclear power would be possible was 'talking moonshine'. But five years after his death in 1937, the first nuclear reactor was in operation.

There's nothing there!

★ ★

FIRST ROCKET

The first rocket was launched more than 700 years ago. No one knows who first invented the rocket, but there are reports that Chinese soldiers were using them in battles before the year 1250. These were solid-fuel rockets, similar to today's fireworks. The first liquid-fuelled rocket was launched in America in 1926 and reached a height of 12.5 metres - about as high as a four-storey building. That's only one-tenth the height of the giant liquid-fuelled Saturn V rocket that launched men to the Moon in the 1960s and 70s.

CAUGHT IN MID-AIR

Catching satellite capsules in mid-air was a tricky technique used in the early years of the space age. Some American 'Discoverer' satellites were used for spying. They took photographs of the Earth's surface as they orbited overhead, and the photographic film was then ejected in a special heat-proof capsule. Aircraft trailing a long loop of wire were supposed to capture the capsule as it floated down to Earth by parachute - but they often missed.

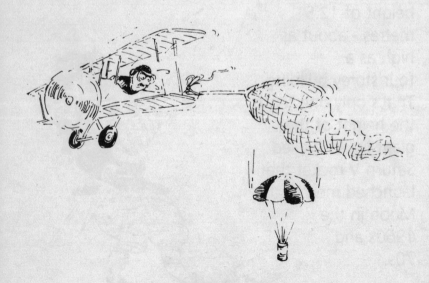

SPACE DOG

The first living creature to orbit the Earth was a dog called Laika. People all over the world were amazed and horrified when the USSR launched its Sputnik 2 satellite in November 1957, because there was a living animal on board. Laika had her own compartment and did not have to wear a space suit, but sadly she died after a week in space. Sputnik 2 itself burnt up as it plunged back to Earth in April 1958. Three years later the Russians put the first human, Yuri Gagarin, into orbit.

BORN IN SPACE

When the Soviet satellite Cosmos 1667 returned to Earth in 1985 there were more passengers on board than when it took off a week earlier. Some baby rats had been born in space. As well as rats, Cosmos 1667 carried monkeys and newts, and 1500 fishes and flies. Its cargo also included some grains of corn and some crocuses. The aim was to study how living things coped with being 'weightless'. Weightlessness (better known as 'free fall') is the condition when something is moving freely in space, without the help of rockets. It feels as though gravity has been switched off, and everything floats about.

CLOCKS IN SPACE

There are clocks in orbit round the Earth which are so accurate they would still be right to the nearest second after 150,000 years. The clocks are installed in a network of satellites which orbit at a height of 20,000 kilometres (12,000 miles). Using special equipment tuned in to time-signals from these satellites, people on the ground can find out exactly where they are, on land or sea or in the air - to the nearest few metres. With this system, called GPS or 'global positioning system', nobody need ever feel lost again.

COASTING ALONG

Spacecraft are the most efficient form of transport - but only in space! Once they have got going and are far away from any planets, spacecraft can travel billions of kilometres without using any fuel at all. They keep on coasting along because there is nothing in space to drag against them and slow them down (unlike on Earth, where everything is slowed by friction or air resistance). But a spacecraft can be slowed down by the pull of the Earth's gravity on its outward journey and speeded up as it returns. And the gravity of the Moon or the Sun - or anything else - can have the same effect (*see* **Roundabout route**, *page 70*).

DOWNSIDE UP

It's easy in space!

There is no 'up' or 'down' in space - all directions feel the same. When a spacecraft is coasting through space, the effects of gravity are cancelled out and everything inside it is 'weightless'. Anything that is not fixed down floats about - even grains of dust and loose crumbs of food. At night astronauts have to be tethered to stop them drifting around as they sleep. One astronaut did not like his sleeping position, so he simply turned upside down - it felt just the same.

RISING AND SETTING

The Sun rises and sets fifteen times a day if you're an astronaut orbiting the Earth. Moving at 27,000 kilometres per hour (17,000 miles per hour), a spacecraft in a low orbit goes round the world in 90 minutes. So for 45 minutes the spacecraft looks down on the sunlit side of the Earth. Then the Sun sets, leaving the craft in the dark for 45 minutes until the next sunrise. Each place on the ground stays in sight for about five minutes as the craft passes overhead.

FLOATING TALL

People in space are up to five centimetres (two inches) taller than they are on Earth. Without the effect of gravity pressing them down, their vertebrae (sections of the spine) move a little further apart. This increases their height. Astronaut Pete Conrad liked being in space because it was the only time he was as tall as his wife was on Earth. But he shrank back to normal as soon as he landed. Other effects of weightlessness, such as your bones gradually getting weaker, do not wear off so quickly, and could be a problem for anyone who stayed weightless for several years.

SUDDEN DEATH

In 1971 three Soviet cosmonauts left the Salyut 1
space station to start their journey back to
Earth. One minute later all three were dead. The
tragedy happened because a valve accidentally
opened and let all the air out of their spacecraft.
Because it is a vacuum - a place with no air -
space is a perilous place for humans to go.
Astronauts and cosmonauts (the Russian name
for astronauts) must spend every moment of
their time in a place which provides its own air
pressure - inside a spacecraft or wearing a
spacesuit. If the cosmonauts from Salyut 1 had
been wearing spacesuits they would have
survived.

DANGER - NO AIR!

FEELING SICK

Half the people who go into space suffer from space-sickness, even if they have never been seasick or airsick before. Space-sickness comes on after a few hours in orbit. It makes astronauts feel ill, and they often have to carry a sick-bag with them as they do their work. Luckily it wears off after three or four days. Nobody knows why some people are affected by space-sickness and others are not.

SPACE RESCUE

In 1973 two American astronauts 'walked' in space and saved a crippled space station worth billions of dollars. The Skylab space station had been damaged when it was launched, so that one of its solar panels came right off and the other one did not open properly. Solar panels are needed to convert energy from sunlight into electricity to power the station. Skylab was saved by astronauts Charles Conrad and Joseph Kerwin, who floated out from the station and managed to tug the jammed solar panel until it opened.

SPIDERS IN SPACE

Spiders called Anita and Arabella became world celebrities when they were taken up to the Skylab space station in 1973. They were taking part in an experiment, suggested by school students, to see if spiders can build webs when they are weightless. At first Anita and Arabella failed to build proper webs as they orbited the Earth, but they tried again and did much better the next time. Unfortunately both spiders died before they could return to Earth, perhaps because they did not have enough to eat or drink.

DOWN TO EARTH

The American Skylab space station crashed to
Earth in a man-made meteorite shower over
Western Australia. It happened in 1979, when
Skylab was no longer occupied. The space
station had been in orbit for six years and had
circled the Earth 35,000 times at a height of
only 450 kilometres (280 miles) above the
surface. There is very little air at that height, but
it was enough to brush against Skylab and bring
about its downfall. No one on the ground was
hurt by falling debris, and an American
newspaper offered a prize for the first person to
find a piece of Skylab on the ground.

FROST AND FIRE

Space shuttle Challenger blew up in mid-air
because it was launched after a frosty night.
Challenger had special rubber rings to stop hot
gas spurting out through a crack where two
parts of its rocket motors join together. But
when rubber gets too cold it loses some of its
springiness. On 28 January 1986 Challenger was
launched after standing out on the launchpad
throughout a frosty night. One of the rubber

★ ★

rings was too cold to work properly. Hot gas escaped and set light to the spacecraft. All seven astronauts died in the fireball that followed.

EXPENSIVE GEAR

Spacesuits for Shuttle astronauts cost more than three million dollars each. Inside the Shuttle astronauts can wear normal clothing, but if they go outside they must put on the complex specially-designed spacesuit. This provides the air pressure they need because there is no air in space, and stops them getting too hot or cold. Radio equipment is built into the suit, and a backpack provides the wearer with enough oxygen and electric power for a six-hour spacewalk. The helmet is like a plastic goldfishbowl and gives a good view of what is going on outside.

SHUTTLE-PECKERS

The launch of a Space Shuttle was held up in 1995 because birds pecked its fuel tank. The birds were woodpeckers that normally drill into trees to get insects to eat

I've always wanted a nest in outer space!

or to make a nesting-hole. Shortly before the Shuttle was due for launch, technicians found that woodpeckers had made more than 50 holes in the foam insulation surrounding the Shuttle's huge fuel tank, which holds 600 tons of liquefied oxygen and 100 tons of liquefied hydrogen. So the Shuttle had to be taken back to its Assembly Building for repair before it could be launched safely.

NOWHERE TO LAND

While Sergei Krikalev and Alex Volkov were in orbit in December 1991, their home country vanished from the face of the Earth. The two cosmonauts were on board the Mir space station. While they were there, the USSR, the country that launched them, was abolished and replaced by a group of new countries. So Krikalev and Volkov went into space as citizens of the USSR, and returned as citizens of the new Russian Federation. Krikalev's stay in orbit had begun in May 1991, when he was accompanied on the journey to Mir by the first British astronaut, Helen Sharman. Sharman stayed a few days in space, but Krikalev remained for a record-breaking ten-month stay.

GOING CHEAP

The Soviet space shuttle only ever made one flight, and was then put up for sale second-hand. The Soviet shuttle, called Buran, looked like the American one. In 1988 it made its first and only flight, which lasted for just two orbits. The spacecraft was flown by automatic pilot, with nobody on board. Later, an advertisement appeared in a magazine offering Buran for sale as scrap. A trial version of Buran, used for testing, was taken to a park in Moscow for use as a restaurant specialising in 'space food'.

Quiz

1   What was the first creature to be launched into orbit round the Earth?
    a)   A newt called Norman
    b)   A fish called Wanda
    c)   A dog called Laika

2   A spacecraft can travel millions of miles through space without using any fuel. Why is this?
    a)   Because there aren't any filling-stations in space
    b)   Because spacecraft just coast along, with nothing to slow them down
    c)   Because the pilot has fallen asleep

3   Why did people in parts of Australia see a spectacular meteorite shower one night in 1979?
    a)   Because the Earth and Moon almost collided
    b)   Because a disused space station fell back to Earth
    c)   Because they had been to a beer-drinking festival

4   You are in orbit in the Space Shuttle and you spill a packet of crisps. What happens to the crisps?

a) They float about all over the place
b) They are eaten by a spider called Anita
c) They disappear down a black hole

5 Who was the first person ever to let off a rocket, and when did they do it?
a) Guy Fawkes on 5 November 1603
b) No one knows who, but it was before the year 1250
c) George Stephenson in 1829

6 Why do astronauts get taller when they are in space?
a) Because space food is so nourishing
b) Because their spacesuits are too tight
c) Because they're not squashed down by gravity any more

7 Why did two astronauts go for a space-walk in 1973?
a) To give their dog Laika some exercise
b) To put right some damage to their Skylab space station
c) To wave to their mums back on Earth

8 Why were two spiders taken into space in 1973?
a) To see if they could still build their webs

    b)   To shoot a scene for the film 'Arachnophobia'
    c)   By mistake because the spacecraft hadn't been dusted
        properly

9 Why are space suits for Shuttle astronauts so expensive?
    a)   Because they have to protect the astronauts from so
        many hazards
    b)   Because astronauts only get their suits from the very
        best tailors
    c)   Because solid gold suits are the only ones strong enough
        for use in space

10 What held up the launch of a Space Shuttle in 1995?
    a)   A squirrel made its nest in one of the rocket motors
    b)   One of the astronauts forgot their packed lunch
    c)   Some birds thought the Shuttle was a tree and started
        pecking it

CHAPTER 2
Mission to the Moon

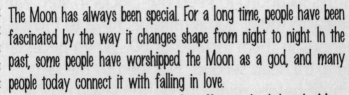

★ ★

The Moon has always been special. For a long time, people have been fascinated by the way it changes shape from night to night. In the past, some people have worshipped the Moon as a god, and many people today connect it with falling in love.

More than 2000 years ago people in China realised that the Moon somehow makes things happen here on Earth. It pulls on the water in the oceans, making tides go in and out. And occasionally the Moon gets between us and the Sun, causing an eclipse – when it gets dark for a minute or two, even in the middle of the day.

When the telescope was invented, astronomers could study the Moon in more detail. They could see mountains on its surface, and began to realise that it is another large, solid world, similar to our own world in some ways, but very different in others. For many years the idea of actually going to the Moon was simply a dream.

Then, in 1969, the dream came true. Neil Armstrong and Buzz Aldrin were the first humans to visit another world. For many people alive at the time, it was the most exciting voyage of discovery of all time. The next step will be to set up a base on the Moon, where visitors from Earth could stay for months or years at a time. But at present no one knows when this will be done.

★ ★

CHANGING DAYS

When dinosaurs roamed the Earth there were only 23 and a half hours in a day. This is because the Earth's rotation is slowing down, so days are getting longer. Ocean tides, caused by the Moon, act like a brake and slow down the Earth's rotation. To keep our clocks in step with the Earth today, some minutes have to have 61 seconds in them instead of 60. When necessary, the extra 'leap second' is added to the last minute before midnight on the last day of July or the last day of December.

STONE CALENDAR?

Stonehenge may have been one of the first astronomical observatories. It was built more than 4000 years ago, in a way that makes some of its giant stones line up exactly with the point where the Sun comes up over the horizon on midsummer's day. People argue about what Stonehenge, and many other stone circles, were actually used for. They could have served as giant calendars, using observations of the Sun and Moon to mark the changes of the seasons, but many people believe they were also religious temples.

FATAL MISTAKE

In ancient China, astronomers were put to death because they did not foretell an eclipse of the Sun. In this sort of eclipse the Sun seems to have a bite out of it, because the Moon is passing in front of it. People thought eclipses would bring bad luck. There is a story that in China in 2137 BC the king's astronomers, called Hsi and Ho, were drunk and had not been taking the measurements that would help predict an eclipse. So when an eclipse happened unexpectedly, Hsi and Ho were beheaded.

MISSING DAYS

People in Britain who went to bed on the second day of September 1752 found it was the fourteenth when they woke up the next morning. But they hadn't spent twelve days asleep. A special law had been passed to change the calendar, so that the days between 2 and 14 September 1752 never happened. This was to bring the calendar back into step with the Earth's movement round the Sun. To stop us getting out of step again we now miss out certain leap years. Leap years, with 366 days instead of 365, normally come round every fourth year, but the year 2100 will be a normal year not a leap year.

NEW MOON

Every time you see a full Moon it is further away than the last one, but only by about two millimetres. This is another result of the effects of tides on the Earth (*see* **Changing days**, *page 32*). So a long time ago the Earth and Moon were quite close. Many astronomers now think that the Moon was formed more than four billion years ago, when a huge meteorite the size of Mars hit the Earth a glancing blow. In this gigantic collision, material from the Earth splashed out into space and eventually became the Moon, which has been getting further and further away from us ever since.

DRY SEAS

There are 'seas' on the Moon, but no water. In 1651 an Italian astronomer called Giovanni Riccioli published a book in which he used the name 'Mare' for the darker patches on the Moon's surface. '*Mare*' (pronounced Ma-ray) is the Latin word for 'sea'. '*Mare Imbrium*' is the 'sea of showers' and '*Mare Nectaris*' the 'sea of nectar'. Today we know there is no water at all on the Moon's surface, but the old names have stuck. You can see some of these 'seas' if you look at the full Moon. They are the darker patches in the pattern often referred to as the 'man in the Moon'.

HIDDEN FROM VIEW

Until 1968 no one had ever seen the far side of the Moon. As it orbits the Earth, the Moon keeps the same face towards us all the time, so we never see the back. In 1959 an unmanned Soviet spacecraft, Luna 3, orbited the Moon and sent back the first photographs of the far side. Nine years later, three US astronauts on the Apollo 8 mission were the first humans to get a direct view of the back of the Moon. The Moon's far side is different from the side we see from Earth - more rugged, with many craters and very little of the 'mare' type of surface (*see previous page*).

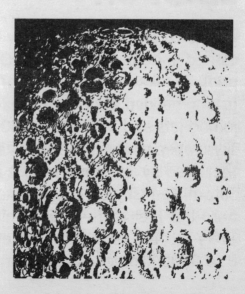

COSTLY JOURNEY

If all the money spent on sending astronauts to the Moon had been laid end to end in the form of one-dollar banknotes, it would reach to the Moon and back seven times. That was the cost of the human race's first-ever exploration of another world. More than half a million people worked on the Apollo project, developing the huge rocket and complex spacecraft needed to escape the Earth's gravity, land twelve astronauts on the Moon, and bring them safely home again.

BLAST-OFF

At launch each huge Saturn V Moon-rocket carried enough fuel to fill an Olympic swimming pool. To take three men out of the Earth's gravity needed a rocket as heavy as eight jumbo-jets and as high as a 40-storey skyscraper. Its main fuel was kerosene, similar to that used by jet airliners. As it blasted off, Saturn V's first-stage rocket motors started to burn this fuel at the rate of thirteen tonnes every second, taking the rocket's speed from 0 to 9600 kilometres per hour (6000 miles per hour). The entire swimming-pool-ful of fuel was used up in only 2.5 minutes.

TOP SPEED

The fastest humans ever were three American astronauts whose Apollo 10 spacecraft touched 39,897 kilometres per hour (24,791 miles per hour) on the way back from orbiting the Moon in May 1969. At that speed they could complete a marathon in four seconds.

The Apollo spacecraft had no brakes. To prevent disaster it used air pressure to slow it down as it hurtled into the Earth's upper atmosphere. Friction with the air made the spacecraft red hot and burned away its special heat shield. The astronauts inside could only relax when the parachutes finally opened for a soft landing in the sea.

CUTTING IT FINE

The Apollo 11 Moon-lander Eagle only had enough fuel for another twenty seconds flying when it made the first-ever landing on the Moon at the end of a three-day journey. If Neil Armstrong had needed half a minute longer to find a suitable spot and land the spacecraft, it would have run out of fuel and crashed. Controllers on Earth were holding their breath; after the landing the commentator told the astronauts: 'You've got a bunch of guys about to turn blue - we're breathing again. Thanks a lot.' Eagle's momentous touch-down took place at 8:17 p.m. Greenwich Mean Time on 20 July 1969. For the first time in history, humans had left Earth and reached another world.

SMALL WORLD

Hold your arm out straight and look at your thumbnail. That's how small the Earth looks when you are on the Moon. In 1969 astronaut Michael Collins saw the Earth as he orbited the Moon and said it was the most beautiful object he had ever seen. It looks like a tiny blue and white blob, as round as a ball, but it shines brightly against the blackness of space. A 'full Earth' seen from the Moon is 50 times brighter than a full Moon is here on Earth.

SILENT WORLD

It's no good shouting for help on the Moon. With no air, sounds can't travel at all, so no one would come to your rescue. Even when they were only a metre apart, astronauts had to talk to each other by radio, using microphones and earphones fixed inside their space suits. This meant that millions of people back on Earth could also listen in to the astronauts' conversations.

PRINTS FROM THE PAST

The footprints that Neil Armstrong and the other astronauts left on the surface of the Moon will still be there in a million years' time - unless a meteor crashes in from space or someone else from the Earth goes to the Moon and messes them up. The Moon has no air, so there is no weather there. It can't rain and no wind can ever blow. So footprints don't get worn away the way they do on Earth. Only a gentle hail of space-dust settles on the Moon's surface.

MOON MIRROR

Astronomers have shone a beam of light at the Moon and seen its reflection from a mirror there. The mirror was a special reflector left on the Moon's surface by the Apollo 11 astronauts. Scientists on Earth sent flashes of laser light to the Moon and timed how long it took for each flash to be reflected back - like waiting to hear an echo if you shout or clap your hands some distance from a cliff or wall. From their measurements the scientists were able to work out exactly how far away the Moon is - to the nearest fifteen centimetres (six inches).

TRAPPING THE SUN

As well as Moon-rock, Apollo astronauts brought part of the Sun back to Earth. Like a boiling cauldron, the Sun blasts out atoms - tiny particles of matter - from its hot atmosphere. These atoms stream out through space, and billions of them collided with a piece of aluminium foil set up on a pole by the astronauts on the Moon. Later they rolled up the foil and brought it back to Earth. Scientists found atoms of helium and neon from the Sun stuck onto the foil.

SAVED BY STICKY TAPE

Plastic bags and sticky tape saved the lives of three astronauts in 1970. When the ill-fated Apollo 13 mission was 300,000 kilometres (200,000 miles) from Earth, it was badly damaged when an oxygen tank exploded. It looked as though the astronauts would be suffocated by a build-up of carbon dioxide before they got home. But then, in best 'Blue Peter' style, people in the Control Room on Earth told them how to make a vital connecting tube out of everyday materials available in the spacecraft. The tube worked, and the astronauts landed safely back on Earth after four hair-raising days in space.

Yes it's lovely. But what we need is ...

KEEP IT COOL

Some of the fuel tanks in the Apollo spacecraft were so well insulated that if you filled one of them with ice it would take more than eight years to melt. And if you had filled one with coffee it would have stayed hot for several years too. Although they stored liquid oxygen and liquid hydrogen, the tanks didn't leak much either. If a car tyre leaked at the same rate as one of these fuel tanks, it would take 30 million years to go flat.

MOON BUGGY

On the last three Apollo missions the astronauts took an electric buggy with them and drove about in it on the Moon. The buggy, called the Lunar Rover, had to be unfolded when they arrived on the Moon's surface. It was powered by batteries and had a top speed over the Moon's rugged surface of eighteen kilometres per hour (eleven miles per hour) - downhill. The Lunar Rover carried astronauts on journeys up to ten kilometres (six miles) from their base, visiting new areas, and collecting samples of moonrock to bring back to Earth.

IN QUARANTINE

The first astronauts to walk on the Moon were
kept in a sealed 'quarantine chamber' for
eighteen days after they landed back on Earth.
Some scientists thought there might be primitive
life on the Moon, in the form of microbes which
might accidentally be brought back to Earth and
could be harmful. So Neil Armstrong, 'Buzz'
Aldrin and Michael Collins were locked away
like people with some deadly infectious disease
- along with a colony of white mice. The mice
and the astronauts stayed healthy, and no sign
of any moon-bugs has ever been found, either
on the Moon itself or on people and spacecraft
that have visited it.

Quiz

1 How high was a Saturn V Moon rocket?
   a) As tall as a 40-storey skyscraper
   b) As high as an elephant's eye
   c) Three times the height of the Man in the Moon

2 What should astronauts do when their spacecraft glows red hot as it comes back to Earth?
   a) Sit tight and wait for it to be over
   b) Get out the fire extinguishers
   c) Call the AA

3 When dinosaurs roamed the Earth, why were days shorter than they are now?
   a) Because dinosaurs didn't have wrist-watches
   b) Because dinosaurs needed a lot of sleep
   c) Because the Earth used to spin more quickly in those days

4 Why did people at Mission Control look blue when Apollo 11 made the first touch-down on the Moon?

a) They were cold because the heating in the Control Centre had broken down

b) They were holding their breath in case Apollo ran out of fuel

c) They were going on to a fancy-dress party

5 Which would make most noise on the Moon, dropping a pin or banging two saucepans together?

a) The saucepans – obviously!

b) The pin, because the saucepans would melt on the Moon

c) Both the same – total silence, because sounds can't travel on the Moon

6 Why were the first astronauts put into quarantine when they got back from the Moon?

a) In case they had picked up any alien moon-bugs

b) To protect them from newspaper reporters

c) Because they hadn't had a bath for a week

7 You are the king's astronomer in ancient China, and an eclipse happens unexpectedly. What do you do?

a) Tell the king he's seeing things

b) Run for your life

c) Pour yourself another drink

8   On your first visit to the Moon, you decide to make a
    soft-landing by parachute. Why is this a bad idea?
    a)   Because a parachute wouldn't work where there is no
         air
    b)   Because the Moon's gravity is so weak you might float
         away into space
    c)   Because you might land on a bit of moonrock and
         sprain your ankle

9   What makes the tide come in and out at the seaside?
    a)   The Earth breathing very slowly
    b)   A big pump in the middle of the sea
    c)   The Moon's gravity pulling on the water

10 What was the Lunar Rover?
    a)   A special spacecraft for flying around the Moon
    b)   A special car for driving on the Moon
    c)   The first dog on the Moon

CHAPTER 3

Exploring other Worlds

1632 was a bad year for the human race! Before then nearly everyone thought that the Earth was a very important place, the centre of the universe. Then in 1632 the Italian scientist Galileo Galilei published a book which showed that the Earth isn't special and important at all. It is just one planet among a family of planets which orbit the Sun. Together they are called the Solar System.

Even with their best telescopes, astronomers could not find out much about the other planets. So when the space age began, special robots were designed which could survive long periods in the cold harsh environment of space. These robot spacecraft did not ever need to return to Earth; they could just send back pictures and other information by radio.

By 1990 robot spacecraft had flown past all the planets in the Solar System except Pluto, taking close-up photographs of their surfaces and discovering fantastic moons and ring systems. Space probes had even made successful landings on the surfaces of Venus and Mars.

Today, more journeys to distant parts of the Solar System are planned or under way, and more exciting discoveries will be made in the years ahead.

STARS WITH LONG HAIR

Thousands of years ago, people found 'wanderers' and 'hairy stars' in the sky. Although they did not have telescopes, people in ancient times knew the night sky much better than most of us do today. They noticed that most of the stars keep their fixed patterns, but a few are 'wanderers'. We call these 'planets', from the Greek word for 'wanderer'. And occasionally they saw small wispy patches in the sky which they called 'long-haired stars'. The Greek for long-haired is *kometes*, so we call these hairy visitors comets.

Get yer 'air cut!

DEADLY SIGHT

When a comet appeared in 1528, some people were so terrified that they died of fright - according to a book written at the time. In olden days people feared comets and thought they brought disaster and bad luck. But the writer who said that people died of fright when they saw the comet of 1528 may have been exaggerating. He also claimed that people saw other strange things in the sky near the comet: axes, knives, swords and a lot of hideous human faces!

BANNED BOOK

A famous astronomy book was banned for 200
years. The book was by Galileo and came out in
1632. One of the characters in it puts forward
good reasons why the Earth must be moving in
orbit round the Sun. But at that time the
teaching of the Roman Catholic Church was
that the Earth did not move, but was fixed at
the centre of the universe. So Galileo was made
to say he didn't really believe what he had
written, and his book was banned. The ban was
lifted in 1832, but it wasn't until 160 years later,
in 1992, that the Pope finally admitted that the
Church had been wrong to punish Galileo.

PLANET WITH KNOBS ON?

When Galileo looked at Saturn through his telescope in 1610, he thought the planet had two companions, fixed to either side like handles. Two years later, these companions had vanished. Galileo was really seeing Saturn's rings, but his telescope wasn't good enough to show exactly what they were. The rings seemed to vanish because they are so thin that they cannot be seen at all when they are edge-on to the Earth - like trying to look at a CD sideways-on.

FIT FOR A KING

If William Herschel had got what he wanted, the planets would now be called Mercury, Venus, Earth, Mars, Jupiter, Saturn ... and 'George'. Herschel was the astronomer who discovered a new planet in 1781. He wanted to name it 'George's Star' in honour of the British king at the time, George the Third. Other people did not like this name, and the planet was eventually christened Uranus, after one of the Greek gods. Since then two more planets, Neptune and Pluto, have been discovered.

ALIEN DIGGERS

A century ago many people believed there were intelligent creatures on Mars. With a powerful telescope, Percival Lowell, an American, thought he could see huge channels on the planet's surface. He wrote about creatures on Mars desperately digging the channels to carry water to make their crops grow, because the planet was drying up and they were in danger of starving. Other astronomers disagreed with him, but many people clung to the idea of 'canals' on Mars. When spacecraft began to visit Mars in the 1960s they found no sign of the channels. Lowell had been mistaken.

MARTIANS INVADE

There was panic in America one day in 1938 when people thought their country was being invaded by Martians, attacking people with death-ray guns. Roads turned into race-tracks as thousands of families left their homes to drive away from the danger area. One woman even tried to kill herself to avoid being captured by the alien invaders. But it was all a mistake, caused by a radio broadcast of the story *War of the Worlds* by H. G. Wells. The broadcast was so realistic that people who switched on late thought it was really happening. Today we know there aren't any signs of life on the planet Mars - but in 1938 people weren't so sure.

ANTI-COMET PILLS

Anti-comet pills were put on sale in 1910 when the Earth was about to pass through the tail of Halley's comet. People panicked and thought the pills would save them from being poisoned by gases from the comet. But it was all a false alarm. A comet's tail is so thin that it is not dangerous. Today air pollution from factories and traffic is much more of a problem than any

comet's tail would be. In any case the anti-comet pills were no good at all - except to make money for the person who made them.

FLAT EARTH?

College students sometimes form 'Flat Earth Societies', for people who refuse to believe that the world is round. In the past many people thought the Earth was flat. Then in the 1520s an expedition sailed right round the world without falling off the edge. And today we've all seen photographs of the round Earth in space. So today most people who join Flat Earth Societies do it for fun, not because they really doubt that the Earth is round.

MINI-PLANETS

I told you it wasn't a giant potato.

The Sun has more than 7000 known planets. Nine of them are large ones, like the Earth or Jupiter, and the rest are much smaller. These mini-planets are called asteroids. The largest asteroid, Ceres, is 900 kilometres across (600 miles), so its surface area is four times smaller than the USA. Some asteroids are chunks of rock only one or two kilometres in size, and there are probably millions more which are so small that they do not show up with telescopes. Most asteroids orbit round the Sun at a distance further than Mars but closer than Jupiter.

BOMBARDED FROM SPACE

The Earth is bombarded by a hundred million high-speed projectiles from space every day. Called meteoroids, these projectiles are tiny grains of grit travelling through the Solar System at speeds up to 72 kilometres per second (45 miles per second). As each one hurtles into the upper atmosphere it burns up, producing a streak of light across the sky which lasts a second or two. This is called a 'shooting star'- although it hasn't really got anything to do with the stars. You might catch a glimpse of a 'shooting star' if you watch the sky for a while on a clear dark night.

NEAR MISS

In 1968 the asteroid Icarus passed the Earth at high speed, only 6,400,000 kilometres (4,000,000 miles) away. By astronomy standards that counts as a very near miss! Icarus is a lump of rock 800 metres across and weighs about 700 million tonnes - enough to do a lot of damage. Luckily astronomers have studied the orbit that Icarus follows and have worked out that this particular asteroid won't collide with the Earth in the near future.

EARTH AT RISK

There's a one in a million chance that an asteroid one kilometre across will collide with the Earth this year - or in any year. That's the estimate astronomers have made after studying a group of asteroids which no longer follow their normal orbits. These asteroids now move on paths which cut across the orbit of the Earth. The impact of a one-kilometre asteroid would make an explosion as large as several hydrogen bombs going off, and leave a crater nearly fifteen kilometres (nine miles) across. There's an even lower chance that a ten-kilometre asteroid could hit the Earth (*see* **Death of the dinosaurs**, *on the next page*).

DEATH OF THE DINOSAURS?

A lump of rock ten kilometres (six miles) across may have crashed into the Earth 66 million years ago and wiped out the dinosaurs. Scientists argue about why the dinosaurs suddenly became extinct. One theory is that a meteorite or asteroid hit the Earth at a speed of several hundred thousand kilometres per hour and threw up so much dust and rock into the air that the whole Earth was cold and dark for months. No plants grew and the dinosaurs starved to death. Not all scientists support this dramatic theory.

RENDEZVOUS IN SPACE

In 1986 five unmanned spacecraft from Earth flew close to Halley's comet. One of them, called Giotto, passed only 600 kilometres (350 miles) from the comet's head. Giotto survived being buffeted by a jet of dust boiling out of the comet, and sent back photographs which showed that Halley's head was a mucky lump of ice and dirt only fifteen kilometres (ten miles) long. When the comet is near the Sun, a tail of gas trails out for millions of kilometres behind this head. Since 1986 Halley's comet has disappeared into the depths of the Solar System. It will return to near the Earth and Sun in about the year 2061.

LIFE ON EARTH?

It's official – there *is* life on Earth. When the Galileo spacecraft flew past planet Earth in 1990 and 1992 (*see* **Roundabout route**, *page 70*) its instruments detected signs of oxygen and methane in Earth's atmosphere. These are tell-tale gases given off by living things. The spacecraft also picked up strange radio signals, showing there might even be *intelligent* life on the planet!

SINKING WORLDS

If all nine planets were put in a huge bowl of water only one of them, Saturn, would float. Whether things float depends on how dense they are - how many kilograms of mass they pack into a given amount of space. Mercury, Venus, Earth and Mars are solid, rocky worlds, dense enough to sink quickly to the bottom. Jupiter, Uranus, and Neptune are giant balls of gas and would sink more slowly in water, as would the tiny planet Pluto. But Saturn, another 'gas giant', is less dense than water. It would float - but with seven-tenths of its volume submerged.

WISH YOU WERE HERE?

If interplanetary tourism ever becomes possible, Venus will probably be the least popular holiday destination. Visitors there would be crushed by the planet's atmosphere, which is 90 times heavier than the Earth's and mainly made of suffocating carbon dioxide gas. The Sun never shines because Venus is permanently blanketed by thick clouds of concentrated sulphuric acid. Under this blanket the surface gets so hot -

460 °C or 860 °F - that metals like lead, tin and zinc would melt there. To make things even more complicated, a day on Venus lasts longer (243 Earth-days) than a year (225 Earth-days).

SLEEPING GIANT

The largest volcano in the Solar System is three times as high as Mount Everest and ten times the size of the largest volcano on Earth. Called Olympus Mons, the volcano is on Mars, and was discovered by the Italian astronomer Giovanni Schiaparelli in 1879. The volcano has not been active recently, but photographs from spacecraft show lava that has solidified on its slopes fairly recently. Some astronomers think Olympus Mons still erupts every 10,000 years or so.

FALSE ALARM

'There is life on Mars - perhaps.' That was the
conclusion drawn from the first experiment
done by the unmanned spacecraft Viking 1 after
its soft-landing on Mars in 1976. Viking
scooped up some Mars soil and put it into a
testing machine designed to find out if any tiny
forms of life were in the soil. The first results
looked hopeful, but they were not definite.
Later tests were disappointing, proving that
there are no signs of life on Mars at the places
where Vikings 1 and 2 landed.

DUSTY WORLD

On Mars, strong winds whip up dust storms
which sometimes cover the entire planet. The
surface of Mars is a desert, covered with
reddish-coloured sand and dust, with loose
boulders lying around. The planet has a very
thin atmosphere made mainly of carbon dioxide
gas (so visitors from Earth would have to wear
spacesuits). The sky is usually a pale orange
colour, but when strong winds blow it is
darkened by swirling storms of dust.

MYSTERY SPOT

Jupiter's 'Great Red Spot' has been a mystery for
300 years. The spot is a patch of slowly-turning
cloud rather like the weather systems
on the Earth that are called anti-cyclones -
except that the one on Jupiter is twice the size
of the whole Earth. Other cloud patterns on
Jupiter change from day to day, so no one is
sure why the Great Red Spot has lasted so long.
You can see the Spot from Earth with a small
telescope.

GASSY GIANT

Jupiter is so big you could fit the Earth inside it 1300 times over. And one of its moons, Ganymede, is larger than the planet Mercury. Jupiter is not made of rock like the Earth. Instead the giant planet is a huge ball of gas - mainly hydrogen and helium. Although it is so large, Jupiter spins faster than the Earth. A day on Jupiter lasts just under ten hours. But Jupiter takes nearly twelve Earth-years to orbit the Sun, so if you lived there, you would have a long wait between birthdays.

RARE COLLISION

In July 1994 a comet crashed into Jupiter - something that only happens once every 1000 years on average. The comet was called Shoemaker-Levy 9 after the people who discovered it. It had broken into a string of at least 21 pieces which hit the planet one after the other at a speed of 60 kilometres per second (37 miles per second). The larger pieces were two kilometres in size. Astronomers watched as the impacts produced fireballs on Jupiter which were larger than the Earth, and left dark patches on the planet's swirling cloud-covered surface.

EDIBLE SATELLITE?

'Better than a lot of pizzas I've seen.' Those were the words of a leading scientist when he saw the first close-ups of Jupiter's moon Io, radioed back to Earth by the spacecraft Voyager 1 in 1979. Voyager found new active volcanoes on Io, blowing out fountains of dust to a height of several hundred kilometres. Coloured dust and lava from volcanoes have given Io its pizza-like appearance.

SMOOTH WORLD

Jupiter's moon Europa is the smoothest world in the Solar System. Although Europa is 3000 kilometres (2000 miles) across, there are no hills or mountains anywhere on its ice-covered surface. The ice is criss-crossed with dark lines, and is so flat that a model of Europa would be as smooth as a snooker ball. If the Earth was as smooth as Europa, its surface would be completely covered by water, with no land showing through at all.

ROUNDABOUT ROUTE

On its six-year journey to Jupiter, the Galileo spacecraft passed three other planets - and two of them were the Earth! Getting from the Earth to Jupiter is an uphill battle against the drag of the Sun's gravity. Galileo followed a spiral route which took it twice round the Sun, passing Venus once and the Earth twice. Gravity from Venus and Earth tugged at the spacecraft as it passed and gave it extra energy, until it was going fast enough to coast across to Jupiter.

Several other spacecraft have used similar
'gravity-assisted' routes for their interplanetary
journeys.

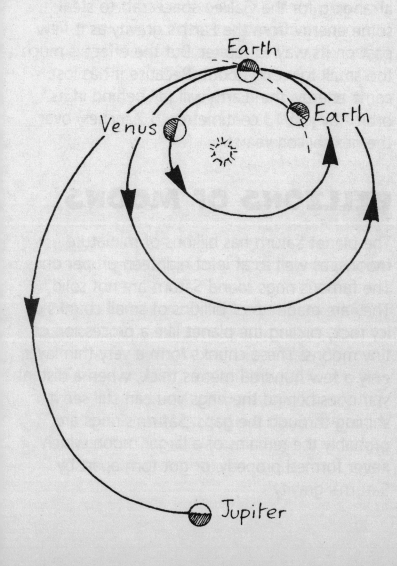

SLOWING THE EARTH

In 1990 and 1992 American scientists made the Earth slow down in its orbit. They did this by arranging for the Galileo spacecraft to steal some energy from the Earth's gravity as it flew past on its way to Jupiter. But the effect is much too small to worry about. Because it has lost some energy, the Earth will fall behind in its orbit - by just 13 centimetres (5.2 inches) over the next billion years!

BILLIONS OF MOONS

The planet Saturn has billions of miniature moons, as well as at least eighteen proper ones. The famous rings round Saturn are not solid. They are made up of billions of small chunks of icy rock, circling the planet like a procession of tiny moons. These chunks form a very thin layer, only a few hundred metres thick; when a distant star goes behind the rings you can still see it shining through the gaps. Saturn's rings are probably the remains of a larger moon which never formed properly, or got torn apart by Saturn's gravity.

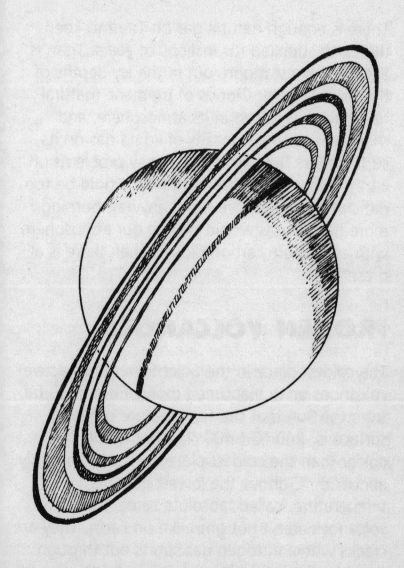

FUEL FROM SPACE

There is enough natural gas on Titan to keep the Earth supplied for millions of years. Titan is Saturn's largest moon, out in the icy depths of the Solar System. Clouds of methane (natural gas) have been seen in its atmosphere, and there may even be oceans of liquid gas on its surface. But Titan won't solve any problems on Earth. Bringing the gas back here would be too difficult and expensive - and anyway, burning more natural gas would pollute our atmosphere with even more carbon dioxide than there is at present.

FROZEN VOLCANOES

The coldest place in the Solar System has active volcanoes on it. Neptune's moon Triton is so far from the Sun that the temperature on its surface is -240 °C (-400 °F). That is 150 °C colder than the coldest place on Earth, and only about 30 °C above the lowest possible temperature, called 'absolute zero'. Triton's volcanoes aren't hot ones like on Earth. They are cracks where nitrogen gas spurts out through the deep-frozen surface, carrying dust to a height of several kilometres before the nitrogen freezes and falls back as snow.

ON TARGET

The spacecraft Voyager 2 was so precisely aimed that after a journey of five billion kilometres (three billion miles) it was only 200 kilometres (125 miles) off course. That's as good as firing an arrow in London and hitting a target the size of a five-pence coin in Paris. Voyager had been travelling for nearly ten years when it reached Uranus. The engineers who control it had planned to make it change course slightly, by

firing small rockets on the spacecraft. But Voyager was so close to its correct course that this was not necessary.

MESSAGE FOR ALIENS

The two Voyager spacecraft carry a video-disc with a recorded message for any 'aliens' they may meet in space. The Voyagers have escaped from the Solar System and will go on coasting through space for millions of years, eventually drifting past distant stars. It is very unlikely that alien creatures (if any exist) will spot one of the Voyagers and capture it, but the video-disc, with sights and sounds from Planet Earth, is there just in case. Instructions on how to play it are given in sign language on the outside.

It's kind of the Earthlings to send us a treat.

Quiz

1 What is an asteroid?
   a) A miniature planet
   b) An astronaut with a head-cold
   c) A type of robot

2 Shooting stars are not really stars at all. What are they?
   a) Bits of rubbish dropped from aeroplanes
   b) Grains of space-dust that burn up in the atmosphere
   c) People who hit the bulls-eye on the rifle range

3 The sky is orange and sand is blowing against the visor of your spacesuit. Where are you?
   a) In the middle of Jupiter's Great Red Spot
   b) Sitting on one of Saturn's rings
   c) Caught in a dust storm on Mars

4 An explorer on Earth finds a rounded hole in the ground, several kilometres wide. What is it likely to be?
   a) A dinosaur's nest
   b) A prehistoric swimming pool
   c) The crater formed by a meteor or asteroid collision

5   What made people panic in America one day in 1938?
   a)   They thought the Martians had landed
   b)   They thought an asteroid was about to hit the Earth
   c)   There was a shortage of coca-cola

6   What would happen if you were sent to Venus without any
    protection?
   a)   You would be flattened to a pancake by the planet's
        gravity
   b)   You would be frozen stiff and your blood would boil
   c)   You would be crushed, roasted and suffocated by the
        atmosphere

7   Why did the Galileo spacecraft take a roundabout six-year
    route from Earth to Jupiter?
   a)   Because it was accidentally launched in the wrong
        direction
   b)   So that it could pick up energy by flying past the Earth
        and Venus
   c)   Because Jupiter wobbled off course while Galileo was on
        its way there

8   Why did William Herschel choose the name 'George's Star'
    for the new planet he discovered in 1781?

a) Because his middle name was George
b) In honour of King George
c) In honour of Boy George

9 You have three children under the age of one, but you've only just passed your third birthday. How is this possible?
a) You live on Jupiter
b) You live on the Moon
c) You're in a space-station orbiting the Earth

10 What would happen if you got too close to one of the volcanoes on Neptune's moon Triton?
a) You would get sucked in
b) You would be vaporised by the heat
c) You would be frozen solid by a blast of icy gas

★ ★ ★ ★ ★ ★ ★ ★ ★ ★ ★

CHAPTER 4

The lives of the Stars

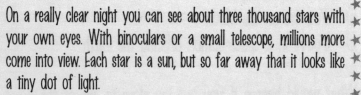

On a really clear night you can see about three thousand stars with your own eyes. With binoculars or a small telescope, millions more come into view. Each star is a sun, but so far away that it looks like a tiny dot of light.

The spacecraft we send out to explore the planets would take millions of years to get to the nearest star. So the only way to find out about stars is to use telescopes and similar instruments. In this way astronomers have been able to work out how stars work – how they are born out of clouds of dust and gas, how they manage to produce so much energy, and how some of them die in spectacular explosions.

The Sun – our own personal star – is vitally important. It lights up our world and supplies the energy that makes plants grow and keeps the Earth warm enough for us to survive.

Not all stars are as well-behaved as the Sun. Some get brighter and dimmer in a regular way, and others have swollen up into red-hot giants. Powerful telescopes pick out tiny stars that spin as fast as tops and are made of super-heavy material. There's even good evidence that a few stars have turned into those invisible pools of ultra-strong gravity called black holes.

HOT AND HEAVY

On the Sun, a person would be as heavy as an elephant is on Earth. The Sun is 330,000 times more massive than the Earth, so its gravity is very strong. If you went to the Sun, gravity would pull you down so hard that your limbs would feel 27 times heavier than they are on the Earth. You probably wouldn't be able to move at all. That wouldn't matter because at a temperature of 6000 °C you would soon be vaporised anyway.

BETTER LATE THAN NEVER

If the Sun stopped producing energy today, we wouldn't know about it for ten million years. A special form of burning - called 'nuclear fusion' - makes the centre of the Sun very hot. But the Sun is so big that heat and light from its centre take ten million years to filter up to the surface. Then it takes another eight minutes for the heat and light to travel across from the Sun to the Earth. So the sunlight that arrives today has taken ten million years - and eight minutes - to get here. Has the Sun already stopped producing energy but we don't know about it yet? Very unlikely - most stars (and the Sun is a typical star) burn steadily for billions of years.

I reckon it's good for another few billion years.

GETTING LIGHTER

In the next five minutes the Sun will get lighter - by a billion tonnes. The Sun 'burns' its hydrogen fuel in a process called nuclear fusion, producing the huge amount of energy that the Sun sends out into space. According to the famous scientist, Albert Einstein, all energy has mass. The mass carried away by the energy that the Sun sends out is four million tonnes every second - close to a billion tonnes every five minutes. Losing mass this fast, how long can the Sun keep going? Read on to find out...

END OF THE WORLD

The Sun will one day grow so big and hot that all the oceans on Earth will boil away. Life will become impossible, unless everyone moves to a distant part of the Solar System. Eventually the giant red Sun will swallow up Mercury and Venus, and possibly the Earth as well. But don't worry, all this won't happen until the Sun begins to run out of fuel - and that won't be for another five billion years.

ZOO IN THE SKY

You can see a crab, a crow, a bull and a lion in the night sky. For centuries people have divided the pattern of stars in the sky into groups called constellations. Many constellations are named after animals, but don't expect them to look much like the animal concerned. A well-known constellation is called the Great Bear, but most people think it looks more like a saucepan! Some constellations, like Leo the lion and Taurus the bull, still have the names that they were given by star-gazers who lived more than three thousand years ago.

LONELY JOURNEY

At the speed of Concorde a journey to the nearest star would take 1.5 million years. After the first three years you would leave the Solar System. Then there would be nothing else to see on the journey, except distant stars. This is just a way of saying that space is very empty. If you made a scale model using a grain of salt to represent the Sun (our local star), its nearest neighbour would be another salt grain, six kilometres (four miles) away.

FINGERPRINTS

Astronomers can tell what stars are made of, just by observing them. The light that each star gives out holds clues about what sort of materials are in that star. Astronomers split the light from the star into a rainbow of colours. Each sort of atom in the star has its own particular pattern of colours, which can be used like a fingerprint. The results show that stars are mainly made of hydrogen atoms, with a smaller proportion of helium and other substances such as oxygen, neon and carbon.

MYSTERY ELEMENT

The gas helium was discovered on the Sun
many years before it was found on Earth. When
the British astronomer Norman Lockyer tested
the Sun's light in 1868, he found it contained a
mystery yellow colour that was not in the
'fingerprint' (*see* **Fingerprints**, *page 85*) of any
substance known on Earth. Lockyer had
discovered a new gas, which he named helium
after the Greek word for sun, *helios*. It was
another 27 years before anyone found any of
the rare gas helium down here on the Earth.

SUPERGIANT

If the star called Betelgeuse was where our sun
is, the Earth's orbit would be inside it.
Betelgeuse is pronounced 'Bettle-gerz' (but
some people call it 'Beetle-juice'). It is a
supergiant star, about 500 times as wide as the
Sun. Placed where our sun is, it would fill the
whole sky, swallowing up Mercury, Venus, the
Earth and Mars. You can see Betelgeuse in the
constellation Orion. Look for an orange-
coloured star that forms Orion's left shoulder as
you face him in the winter night sky. Our sun
will one day grow to be nearly as big as
Betelgeuse (see **End of the world**, *page 83*).

NEW STAR

On 24 February 1987, a new star appeared. The
first person to notice was a Canadian
astronomer called Ian Shelton, working at an
observatory in Chile. What he saw was a
supernova, actually an old star which had
suddenly flared up millions of times brighter and
was blowing itself to pieces. Heavyweight stars
do this when they are running out of fuel at the
end of their lives. This supernova, officially called

SN 1987A, was the first one bright enough to be seen without a telescope since the year 1604. It has now died away and become invisible again.

HEAVY STUFF

Imagine a material so heavy that a matchbox full of it would weigh ten thousand million tonnes - that's what some stars are really made of. If all the people on Earth ganged together to try to lift the matchbox, it would still be too heavy. Stars made of this material are called 'neutron stars'. They are the leftover remains of ordinary stars that have grown old and exploded.

LITTLE GREEN MEN

'Project Little Green Men' was the codename of an experiment to find the source of a strange clicking sound from space, picked up by a radio telescope in 1967. The clicks were so regular that people thought they might be tapped out by real-life aliens. But it soon turned out that the ticking doesn't come from any living things. Certain fast-spinning stars, called pulsars, lash the Earth with a beam of radio waves each time they rotate, producing the steady series of clicks.

This should confuse the Earthlings.

STAR-STUFF

If some stars didn't end their lives by exploding, you wouldn't be reading this book. The tiny particles (called atoms) of substances like carbon and oxygen, are only made inside stars. So carbon and oxygen atoms found on the Earth must have been made inside stars which existed long ago. Some of these stars exploded (*see* **New star**, *page 87*), blowing out clouds of dust

and gas from which the Solar System later formed. So without these exploding stars there could be no carbon and oxygen on Earth. And without these important elements, there could be no book and no people to read it, because all living things have atoms of carbon and oxygen in them.

EXPLODING CRAB

When a star exploded in the group called 'The Crab', no one on Earth knew about it until 5000 years later. Light rays from the exploding star set off at once, travelling at a speed of 300,000 kilometres (186,000 miles) every second. This is 400,000 times faster than Concorde, but even at such a high speed the light rays took 5000 years to reach the Earth. Before they arrived, no one on Earth could possibly know that the star had exploded.

BLACK HOLE

The nearest black hole to the Earth is probably a star called Cygnus X-1. A heavyweight star has collapsed under its own gravity to form a tiny point, surrounded by a pool of gravity so strong that not even light can escape from it. That's why it is called a 'black hole'. Of course astronomers cannot see the black hole itself, but dust and gas from a nearby star is sucked into it and gives off X-rays as it goes. These tell-tale X-rays have been picked up by a special X-ray telescope in orbit round the Earth.

ANOTHER SOLAR SYSTEM

Three planets have been discovered in orbit round a distant star called B1257+12. Two of these planets are about three times as heavy as the Earth, and the third is a baby one, about the same weight as our Moon. B1257+12 is a very odd star that spins round like a top 161 times every second. It is possible that many other stars have their own families of planets, but planets do not give off any light of their own, so it is

difficult for astronomers to observe them in orbit round other stars.

LISTENING IN

For more than 30 years, astronomers in various countries have tried to pick up radio signals from 'Intelligent Beings' in other parts of our galaxy. So far they have had no success. In the 1990s a project called Project Phoenix is using some of the world's largest radio telescopes to tune in to about a thousand different stars. The project's organisers hope that some of these stars may have planets with creatures on them who regularly use radio or television, just as we do on Earth. If so, Project Phoenix should be able to listen in to them.

Quiz

1 If the Sun was a million times further away than it actually is, what would it look like?
   a) Any other ordinary star
   b) The full Moon
   c) You wouldn't be able to see it at all

2 What are stars made of?
   a) Mainly rocks and stones
   b) Mainly hydrogen gas
   c) Mainly green cheese

3 What does the word 'supernova' refer to?
   a) An exploding star
   b) The rocket used to launch interplanetary spacecraft
   c) A powerful brand of washing powder

4 What is Cygnus X-1?
   a) A Martian football team
   b) A top-secret new fighter plane
   c) A mysterious source of X-rays in the sky

5 What are the scientists who work on Project Phoenix hoping to do?
   a) Pick up radio and TV stations on distant planets
   b) Send messages to any inhabitants of Pluto
   c) Pick up the next episode of Neighbours before anybody else

6 What might a black hole look like?
   a) Water going down the plug-hole of your bath
   b) A spinning, flashing light
   c) You can't see it because it's black

7 Where were the carbon and oxygen atoms in your body originally made?
   a) In the mud at the bottom of the sea
   b) In volcanoes which erupted millions of years ago
   c) In stars which exploded before the Earth formed

8 What is Betelgeuse?
   a) The name of Saturn's smallest moon
   b) The name of a star in the Orion group
   c) The name of Captain Marvel's cat in Startrek

9 How was the element helium discovered?
   a) By an astronaut on the back of the Moon
   b) By an astronomer observing the Sun
   c) By a fingerprint expert at Scotland Yard

10 What is a pulsar?
    a) A star that spins and ticks
    b) An interstellar spacecraft
    c) A gang of Little Green Men

CHAPTER 5

The deeper universe

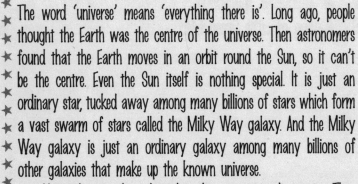

The word 'universe' means 'everything there is'. Long ago, people thought the Earth was the centre of the universe. Then astronomers found that the Earth moves in an orbit round the Sun, so it can't be the centre. Even the Sun itself is nothing special. It is just an ordinary star, tucked away among many billions of stars which form a vast swarm of stars called the Milky Way galaxy. And the Milky Way galaxy is just an ordinary galaxy among many billions of other galaxies that make up the known universe.

New telescopes have brought other surprising discoveries. They show that the universe is changing, gradually swelling up like a balloon being blown up. By picking up light-rays that have been travelling through space for millions of years, powerful telescopes show what the universe was like long ago. Astronomers have become time travellers, who can see into the past.

But no one can see into the future, and at present astronomers cannot tell whether the universe will one day come to an end. You'll have plenty of time to finish reading this book, though, because the end of the universe, if it does ever come, is still many billions of years away in the future!

TIME TRAVEL

On a clear night in the autumn you can see two million years back in time. If you live in the northern hemisphere, wait for a really clear dark night, with no moon. Then use a star-map to find the constellation (pattern of stars) called Andromeda. Look for the very pale patch of light that is the Andromeda galaxy. It's another group of billions of stars, similar to our own galaxy, but so far away that the light it sends out takes two million years to reach Earth. So we say that Andromeda is 'two million light-years away'. If you look at the galaxy tonight, you see it as it was two million years ago.

If you live in the southern hemisphere look for the Magellanic Clouds instead. The Large Cloud is 150,000 light-years from the Earth, and the Small Cloud 200,000 light-years away.

COUNTING STARS (1)

If you started to count the stars in our own galaxy - the Milky Way - it would take you three thousand years to get to the end, counting at the rate of one a second. There are about a hundred billion stars in the galaxy, a number which can be written as 100,000,000,000, or as 1×10^{11}. They are arranged in a flat cloud with spiral arms. Our Sun is a typical one of the Milky Way's stars, about half-way out from the centre.

Fifty-two million, three hundred and six thousand, two hundred and sixty-eight. Fifty-two million three hundred...

COUNTING STARS (2)

To count all the stars in the universe you would have to get everyone on Earth to help. Even then, the job would take 50,000 years. Astronomers have not had time to count all the galaxies that are within the range of their most powerful telescopes, so they have to make an estimate. The result is that there may be as many as a hundred billion galaxies, each one made up of about a hundred billion stars. So that's a total of ten thousand billion billion stars (a 1 with 22 noughts after it) - more than the number of salt grains in all the salt used in the world this century.

EXPANDING UNIVERSE

The universe is bigger today than it was yesterday. Astronomers can tell whether a distant galaxy is moving by testing the colour of the light it sends out. If the galaxy is moving towards the Earth, its light is bluer than expected. If it is moving away, the light has a 'red-shift' - it is redder than expected. Astronomers have found that all the galaxies in the sky are moving away from ours (apart from one or two nearby ones: *see* **Galactic impact**, *below*). And the further away a galaxy is, the faster it is running away. So we seem to be living in an expanding universe.

GALACTIC IMPACT

Our galaxy, the Milky Way, is heading for a collision with its neighbour, the Andromeda galaxy. Almost all galaxies are moving away from each other (that's why astronomers talk about the 'expanding universe'), but Andromeda is an exception. At present it is two million light-years away (*see* **Time travel**, *page 97*), but it is heading our way. It will collide and merge with our own galaxy in about five billion years time - but our descendants will have other things to worry about at that time (*see* **End of the world**, *page 83*).

GREAT ATTRACTOR

Our galaxy is being pulled through space at a speed of two million kilometres per hour (1.3 million miles per hour) by a mysterious force which astronomers call the 'Great Attractor'. Nobody is sure what the Great Attractor is. To exert enough gravity to pull our galaxy, and its neighbours, at such a high speed the Attractor must be as heavy as ten thousand ordinary galaxies added together. Clouds of dust in our own galaxy block the view in the direction where the Great Attractor should be, so it cannot be seen through a telescope.

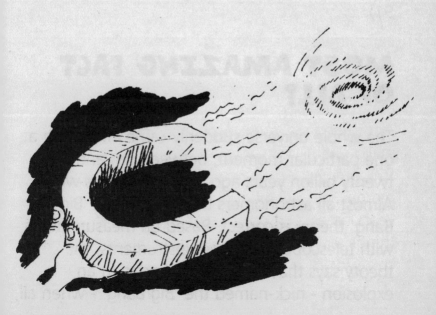

DISTANT BEACONS

There are beacons in the depths of the universe which let astronomers see back almost to the beginning of time. The beacons are called quasars. A single quasar can shine thousands of times more brightly than a whole galaxy, so it can be seen from a huge distance away. Light from the most distant quasars takes so long to reach the Earth that it must have started its journey when the universe was young - only a tenth of the age it is now. Many astronomers think a quasar is a super-massive black hole at the centre of a galaxy (see **Black hole**, *page 91*).

MOST AMAZING FACT OF ALL?

The whole universe suddenly came into being at one particular moment, between ten and twenty billion years ago - no one knows why. Almost all astronomers believe that the 'Big Bang' theory is correct. Based on measurements with telescopes and other instruments, the theory says that the universe began in an explosion - nick-named the 'Big Bang' - when all the matter and energy of the universe suddenly appeared from nowhere, squeezed into a space no larger than an egg. Since then the universe has been expanding and cooling down, forming the galaxies, stars and planets that we see today.

IN THE DARK

The universe was pitch dark for more than half a billion years in its early days. Astronomers believe that a million years after the 'Big Bang', the universe had cooled down so that it was no longer white hot or even red hot. A dark age began and lasted until the first stars lit up, some time before the universe's billionth birthday. Stars form very slowly, when a cloud of gas is pulled together by its own feeble gravity. The gas gets hotter until a point is reached where the star begins to shine.

SITE RESERVED FOR FUTURE GALAXY

COSMIC TV

You can pick up the 'Big Bang' on your television set at home. Switch on the television when there's no station broadcasting, and you see a pattern of dancing dots on the screen. Most of these dots come from the set itself, but a few of them come from the 'Big Bang'. The 'bang' made a 'big flash' of radiation which still fills the universe, although it has gradually changed from light into radio waves. Your television aerial picks up some of these waves and uses them to form some of the dots on the blank screen.

ANCIENT ATOMS

Some of the atoms in your body are almost as old as the universe. Four-fifths of the human body is water, and every tiny particle of water contains two atoms of the gas hydrogen. Astronomers believe that all the hydrogen atoms in the universe were formed only 300,000 years after the Big Bang, when the universe was only one fifty-thousandth of its present age. Before that, there weren't any atoms at all. Since then some hydrogen atoms have got burned up

inside stars - providing the energy to make the stars shine - but others, including the ones in your body, have survived unchanged for billions of years.

END OF THE UNIVERSE

Nobody knows how the universe will end. It may be that the galaxies will go on spreading out until, after many billions of years, the stars have all burnt out and the universe is cold and dead. Or it may be that gravity is strong enough to stop the expansion of the universe, and make it shrink back until everything collapses together in a 'big crunch' - after which it might start all over again. To find which possibility is correct, astronomers need to know how much material there is in the whole universe, and that is uncertain at present.

ALL ALONE?

The Earth is the only place in the whole universe with living things on it - as far as we know at present. Astronomers have used telescopes and spacecraft to search for signs of life on other planets and moons and in other parts of the galaxy, but with no success. But many scientists believe that lots of other stars have families of planets. And with so many stars to choose from, there could be millions of planets in distant parts of the universe where 'alien civilisations' exist at this moment. And who knows - could there even be a distant planet where some strange creature at this very moment is reading some alien version of a book of Amazing Facts about Space?

★ ★ ★ ★ ★ ★ ★ ★ ★ ★ ★

Quiz

1 What is the Great Attractor?
   a) A huge magnet on the Moon
   b) A force pulling our galaxy through space
   c) A powerful machine used by farmers

2 An astronomer sees a very bright spot of light at the centre of a distant galaxy. What is it?
   a) A laser
   b) A quasar
   c) A speck of dust on the telescope lens

3 How did astronomers discover that the universe is expanding?
   a) By visiting distant galaxies
   b) By asking Einstein
   c) By testing the light that comes from distant galaxies

4 Andromeda is the name of . . . what?
   a) One of the constellations in the night sky
   b) A type of chocolate bar
   c) Donald Duck's girl-friend

★ ★ ★ ★ ★ ★ ★ ★ ★ ★ ★

5 X, Y and Z are three people having an argument. Who is right?
   a) X, who says the Earth is at the centre of the universe
   b) Y, who says the Sun is at the centre of our galaxy
   c) Z, who says the Sun is at the centre of the Solar System

6 Four-fifths of your body is made of . . . what?
   a) Water
   b) Bone
   c) Polyunsaturated fat

7 If you went to the centre of our galaxy what might you find there?
   a) An alien civilisation
   b) A super-massive black hole
   c) The end of the rainbow

8 Where do stars come from?
   a) They form from a cloud of gas
   b) They just pop up from nowhere
   c) They are thrown out of quasars

9 What does it mean when we say the galaxy in Andromeda is two million light-years away?
   a) It disappeared two million years ago
   b) It has two million stars in it
   c) Light rays take two million years to get from it to us

10 What is the big crunch?
   a) A possible end of the universe
   b) What happens when two stars collide
   c) A breakfast cereal

Quiz Answers

CHAPTER 1, (P 28)

1 - c,   2 - b,   3 - b,   4 - a,   5 - b,   6 - c,
7 - b,   8 - a,   9 - a,   10 - c

CHAPTER 2, (P 48)

1 - a,   2 - a,   3 - c,   4 - b,   5 - c,   6 - a,
7 - The choice is yours. I would go for b,
8 - a,   9 - c,   10 - b

CHAPTER 3, (P 77)

1 - a,   2 - b,   3 - c,   4 - c,   5 - a,   6 - c
7 - b,   8 - b,   9 - a,   10 - c

CHAPTER 4, (P 93)

1 - a,   2 - b,   3 - a,   4 - c,   5 - a,   6 - c
7 - c,   8 - b,   9 - b,   10 - a

CHAPTER 5, (P 108)

1 - b,   2 - b,   3 - c,   4 - a,   5 - c,   6 - a
7 - b,   8 - a,   9 - c,   10 - a

★ ★ ★ ★ ★ ★ ★ ★ ★ ★ ★ ★

Index